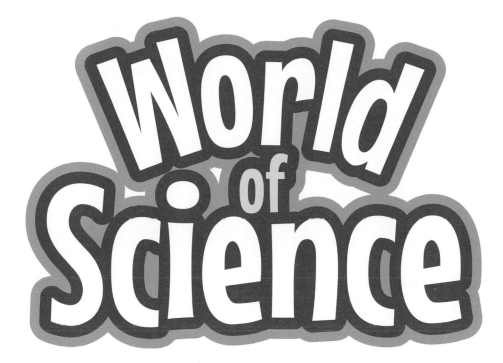

World of Science

Adventures in the Green Movement

Edited by

Karen Kwek

WS Education

NEW JERSEY · LONDON · SINGAPORE · BEIJING · SHANGHAI · HONG KONG · TAIPEI · CHENNAI · TOKYO

Published by

WS Education, an imprint of
World Scientific Publishing Co. Pte. Ltd.
5 Toh Tuck Link, Singapore 596224
USA office: 27 Warren Street, Suite 401-402, Hackensack, NJ 07601
UK office: 57 Shelton Street, Covent Garden, London WC2H 9HE

National Library Board, Singapore Cataloguing in Publication Data
Name(s): Kwek, Karen, editor.
Title: Adventures in the Green Movement / edited by Karen Kwek.
Other Title(s): World of science ; 11.
Description: Singapore : WS Education, [2022]
Identifier(s): ISBN 978-981-12-4168-0 (hardcover) | 978-981-12-4190-1 (paperback) |
    978-981-12-4169-7 (ebook for institutions) | 978-981-12-4170-3 (ebook for individuals)
Subject(s): LCSH: Green movement--Comic books, strips, etc. |
    Green movement--Juvenile literature. | Environmentalism--Comic books, strips, etc. |
    Environmentalism--Juvenile literature. | Graphic novels.
Classification: DDC 363.7--dc23

British Library Cataloguing-in-Publication Data
A catalogue record for this book is available from the British Library.

Published by arrangement by ENGLISH CORNER PUBLISHING PTE LTD

Design and layout: Loo Chuan Ming

Printed in Singapore

What is the green movement?

From the 19th century onwards, people began noticing that advances in technology were changing the physical environment in big ways. Today's green movement, also known as the environmental or ecological movement, started in the 1950s and includes a wide variety of solutions aimed at addressing environmental issues.

Why should we be concerned about plastic waste and noise pollution? How can we manage resources like water and electricity responsibly? Plant a tree, make recycled paper, and turn your food scraps into fertiliser! From recycling tips to eco-friendly sources of energy, be inspired to make your own lifestyle greener!

Experience a world of
interactive discoveries!

Scan to watch a video on activating AR in 3 easy steps.

1 Download the SnapLearn app.

2 Activate by scanning this book's barcode. Then, tap on the book cover image on your screen.

3 Wherever you see this icon, scan the whole page.

Contents

Losing Our Forests

Striking a Balance

Many countries have laws for sustainable forest management. This protects the long-term health of forests by ensuring that timber can be harvested only from certain areas or at certain times, so that the forest can regrow or be replanted.

Shouldn't we protect our forests? Forests support the ecological system and are home to many animals.

They play a role in purifying the air. They help stabilise the climate and enrich the soil with nutrients.

Right.

Why do people still cut down trees and destroy forests?

Because trees provide us with wood for making paper and furniture, and building houses.

But we are losing our forests at an alarming rate!

Yes, we should play our part to save the world's forests.

What can we do?

We can use less paper, buy items made of recycled wood, and make sure that our forestry practices are sustainable.

Plant Them Back
One strategy in sustainable forestry is to make sure that only trees of the same species and age are cut down in a certain area. This area is then replanted with the same number and species of trees.

Part of the Water Cycle

Trees absorb underground water with their roots and release it back into the environment through their leaves in the form of water vapour. This process is called transpiration.

Deforestation Damage

10

Increased Greenhouse Gas Emissions

Carbon dioxide, methane and nitrous oxide are examples of greenhouse gases – gases that trap and hold heat in the atmosphere. Trees absorb carbon dioxide and release oxygen when they make food, but human activities such as burning and deforestation increase the concentration of greenhouse gases in Earth's atmosphere.

Acidic Oceans

Deforestation can result in higher carbon dioxide levels in the atmosphere. When too much carbon dioxide dissolves in seawater, oceans become acidic, endangering aquatic life. For example, acidic seawater slows down the growth of coral and thus affects the ecosystem of the ocean floor.

Debris Flow Disasters

Unplanned deforestation leaves the ground exposed, without tree roots to hold soil in place. During the rainy season, soil erosion on slopes and steep surfaces can cause landslides.

Hazy Days

Low Visibility

Haze consists of soot and dust particles, carbon dioxide and other gases. The tiny pollutant particles scatter light, thus reducing our ability to see our surroundings clearly. Severe haze can bring traffic to a standstill, because it is dangerous to drive when visibility is poor.

How long until the haze disappears?

Haze can last for a long time. Let's hope it's gone by morning. Goodnight!

Teacher! Teacher!

What is going on?

Matt is having trouble breathing!

Okay, get your inhaler from your backpack, Matt.

Why does Matt need an inhaler?

Haze particles can be small enough to enter our lungs when we breathe. People with heart or lung conditions, like Matt who has asthma, are particularly sensitive to air pollution.

13

Hazy Days

Haze in the City

Fog occurs when moist air cools and condenses into tiny water droplets suspended in the air. Sometimes, the haze in urban areas is a mixture of naturally occurring fog and air pollution from human activities such as burning or construction.

The inhaler will deliver medication through his mouth to his airways and lungs. He should be fine!

I hope so!

Inhaling haze is like inhaling smoke – it can irritate your nose and throat. Long-term exposure to toxic particles in haze can contribute to lung diseases such as bronchitis and lung cancer.

Air pollutants can even cause skin irritation, rashes, redness or itching.

Haze is really terrible!

If we had foreseen this haze, we would have postponed the camping trip and remained indoors.

Oh well, until the haze blows over, we'll stay and look after you, Matt!

Thank you!

Recurring Problem

Haze pollution caused by the burning of large tracts of forested land in Indonesia regularly affects several Southeast Asian countries, including Indonesia, Malaysia, Singapore and Brunei. Health warnings are issued during periods of severe haze. People are encouraged to remain indoors or wear protective masks when outdoors.

Haze

Haze is usually caused by human activities. Dust from construction sites, fumes from vehicle exhaust pipes, factory smoke, and smoke from the burning of rubbish can all cause haze.

The greater the concentration of particles suspended in the air, the thicker the haze. Very severe haze can block out so much sunlight that it slows down crop growth and decreases yield.

Hazy conditions reduce visibility, making traffic congestion and road accidents more likely. Pedestrians should exercise extra care when crossing roads during a haze.

15

Hazy Days

Rain That Destroys

One rainy season in a village in the countryside...

Wow!

Dad! Mum!

There are so many dead fish in the pond! We can take some home to eat.

Rain That Destroys

Acidic or Alkaline?

The pH scale is a rating of 0–14 for how acidic or alkaline a solution is. The neutral pH value is 7. Any value below 7 is considered acidic; any value above 7 is considered alkaline. Clean, safe rainwater is slightly acidic, with a pH value of around 5. Acid rain, however, has a pH value of about 4.

Nasty Chemistry

Vehicle exhaust fumes and smoke from industrial facilities contain sulphur dioxide and nitrogen oxides. When combined with water and oxygen, these air pollutants react chemically to form sulphuric acid and nitric acid in the atmosphere. Acidic droplets in clouds then fall as rain, snow or hail.

There are many factories nearby releasing exhaust fumes into the air. A chemical reaction between water vapour and each of these gases results in the formation of acid rain.

To prevent acid rain, we can replace fossil fuels with clean sources of energy, such as wind or solar power. Growing acid-resistant crops, such as camphor or citrus trees, would also reduce the impact of acid rain on food sources.

The issue of acid rain can only be solved by everybody working together. It's going to take time.

I'm afraid not, but don't worry! Until the situation improves, we'll provide you with food and water.

Isn't there a faster way?

Thanks!

Health Risks

Acid rain itself causes more damage to the environment than to human beings. However, the air pollutants that cause acid rain can be harmful if inhaled over a long period of time. They increase the risk of lung diseases such as bronchial asthma (right) and lung cancer.

Acid Rain

The burning of fossil fuels such as coal, oil and natural gas releases harmful substances that combine with water vapour in the atmosphere to form acid rain.

Acid rain dissolves mineral compounds in soil, removing calcium, magnesium and potassium from the top layers. Without the nutrients that they need to thrive, plants and trees wither and die.

Acid rain can corrode construction materials such as metal and paint. It has damaged a large number of buildings and sculptures.

Rain That Destroys

Plastic Graveyard

That's not all... Microplastics are too small to be retrieved from the ocean. They enter marine creatures and eventually find their way into human bodies through our diet.

Oh no!

Besides causing internal blockages, plastic bags that we eat by mistake make us feel full. Without real food in our bodies, we eventually starve to death.

But how could you mistake plastic bags for food?

To us, floating plastic bags look a lot like delicious jellyfish!

I feel awful that human-made plastics are killing your friends!

Tiny organisms that grow on plastic waste, such as algae, can smell like food to animals.

Shoo... Don't eat that!

Why do seabirds eat plastic waste?

Marine and coastal plastic waste is really harmful.

23

Plastic Graveyard

Say "No" to Single-Use Straws
If we don't change how we have been making and using plastics, the total weight of plastics in the oceans could be more than that of all the fish by the year 2050. Many eateries and beverage sellers have stopped giving out plastic straws.

Plastics are widely used because they are cheap to produce.

But wildlife is paying the price.

We humans must learn to use less plastic, and dispose of it properly.

Right! That would save many animal lives.

That's cool! I'm feeling much better. Thanks for your help. I need to go back to the ocean now.

One more thing… Turtles, fish and seabirds aren't the only ones suffering… Whales are also victims of plastic waste.

Yes! A whale in Thai waters died after accidentally eating 80 plastic bags.

I hear you… We'll cut down on our use of plastics for sure!

Bye!

Bye!

Reusable Alternatives

Consider switching to straws made of stainless steel or glass. They can be washed and reused many times, helping to reduce plastic waste.

How to Reduce Plastic Waste

Shop the Eco-friendly Way
Fold up and store the plastic bags that were used to carry home your groceries, so that you can reuse them on your next shopping trip. Even better, switch to string or fabric reusable bags.

Drink Up!
We all need to drink plenty of water every day. Carry around your own reusable water bottle instead of disposable plastic drink bottles.

Recycle Everything
When you are shopping, try to choose non-plastic items and packaging. Before throwing things away, check and sort them, recycling as much as you can. Then properly dispose of items that cannot be reused.

What's All That Noise?

Uncle Ken, you have very dark eye circles.

There's a construction project near the hospital. It's so noisy that I haven't been able to sleep well.

Did you know that noise can be a form of pollution? Because we have grown accustomed to them, we are usually not bothered by city noises such as traffic sounds and loud music, but when noise interferes with our ability to rest or stay on task, it is considered noise pollution.

Ah yes, construction sounds, such as the hammering of a pile driver, can be deafening!

As city life gets busier and busier, noise pollution from construction and transport is becoming more and more severe.

Sound Facts

Noises are sounds that we find annoying or unpleasant. The constant hum of machines or the ear-splitting pop of firecrackers are examples of noise pollution. A living environment that is too noisy can be harmful to our health in the long run.

Poor Planning
Noise pollution can be worsened by poor urban planning, such as when housing is built too close to major roads or industrial areas.

How Does Noise Pollution Damage Our Health?

Exposure to loud noise can trigger a type of headache known as migraine, which can also cause eye pain and blurred vision.

Constant noise is distracting and interferes with concentration. It can disrupt thought, speech, work and learning processes.

Noise pollution can disrupt our sleep, resulting in tiredness and irritability. High levels of noise pollution are associated with increased stress responses, such as high blood pressure, rapid heart rate and greater risk of heart disease.

Power Down, Please!

Power Down, Please!

Power Supply

Power is energy, especially electricity, that is obtained from a fuel source. Electricity is needed to power many modern devices, from refrigerators to computers. The cheapest way to generate power is by burning fossil fuels such as coal, natural gas or oil. This method of generating power is also the most hazardous to the environment.

Power Down, Please!

Energy-Saving Lights

The first light bulbs were incandescent, meaning that light is produced by heating up a thin wire inside the bulb. Most of the energy consumed by incandescent bulbs, however, goes into generating heat, not light. In contrast, light-emitting diode (LED) bulbs (left) produce light without wasting much energy in the form of heat.

Power-Saving Life Hacks

Do not keep your refrigerator doors open longer than necessary. Check the compartment seals to make sure that the refrigerator is well insulated. If frost has formed in the freezer compartment, turn off the appliance to melt and remove the frost. These tips help ensure that no energy is wasted keeping your food cool or frozen.

When using screen devices, keep the volume and brightness at the lowest levels necessary. Instead of putting appliances on standby mode, switch them off when they are not in use.

Did you know that a device plugged into a wall socket continues to draw a small charge unless electricity is switched off at the socket? When appliances are not in use, switch them off at the socket or unplug them.

Every Precious Drop

Water is essential to crop growing and animal farming. We also need water for washing and keeping clean.

We should all consider ways to use less water.

What are the advantages of saving water?

It helps preserve existing water sources and reduce the negative effects of drought.

If people minimise access to water sources such as rivers and underground rock layers that store water, we can also reduce environmental pollution.

Isn't water a renewable resouce? Won't it always return to the planet in one form or another?

Yes, water returns to the planet through the water cycle, but it is not always returned to the same location or in the same quantity or quality.

Three States

Water exists in three states: as a solid, liquid or gas. Ice (right) is the solid form of water. Water vapour is the gaseous form. At temperatures of 0 degrees Celsius or higher, ice melts into liquid water. Water boils at 100 degrees Celsius, turning into water vapour.

The water cycle is the continuous movement of water in Earth's atmosphere. Evaporation is the process by which liquid water turns into vapour. Condensation refers to the cooling of warm vapour into water droplets. Water droplets in clouds fall to the ground in a process called precipitation. Then the cycle is repeated.

Suddenly...

I've brought water!

Crisis relief workers have brought water to the drought area...

Okay, Ryan, get to work!

Huh? What work?

I signed you up as a volunteer to carry water to nearby homes!

Water, Water Everywhere...

Although water covers almost three quarters of Earth's surface, 97 percent of it is saltwater and unsuitable for humans to drink. Of the remaining 3 percent that is freshwater, some is polluted, and more than half is frozen away in icecaps and glaciers. Less than 0.5 percent of Earth's water is suitable for drinking.

Water-Saving Tips

Fix any dripping taps, so that water is not wasted. Do not leave the tap or shower running while you are brushing your teeth, soaping your hands or lathering up in the shower.

Raising animals for meat and dalry products requires more water than growing the equivalent yield of vegetables in weight. Reducing meat and dairy consumption helps save water resources.

A standard showerhead releases about 9–10 litres of water per minute. Make it a habit to take shorter showers, and switch to a low-flow showerhead. Water used to wash fruit or vegetables can be reused to water plants.

Green Rides

The Netherlands is a bicycle kingdom! Bikes are everywhere!

This is a relatively flat country, without many mountains. It is also quite densely populated; towns tend to be near one another, making bicycles a good transport option.

Cycling is promoted as a symbol of Dutch culture and an eco-friendly means of transport.

How else does the Dutch government encourage people to cycle instead of drive?

Towns and cities are planned with the needs of cyclists in mind. The government maintains a continuous network of cycle paths, all clearly signposted and well lit.

Wow, that sure helps make cycling safe and enjoyable!

Bicycle Paths

The Netherlands has a total of some 35,000 kilometres of cycle paths! Some are beside main roads (right), but many are exclusively for bicycles and closed to motorised traffic.

Cycling Culture
In the Netherlands, children are introduced to cycling from a young age. No special equipment is required. Most people ride around in casual or work outfits, and cycling helmets are a rare sight.

Benefits of Cycling

Cycling is an eco-friendly means of transport.
Unlike motorised vehicles, bicycles do not generate greenhouse gas pollutants.

Switching to bicycles reduces the number of motorised vehicles on the roads, easing traffic congestion and reducing fatal road accidents.

Cycling is an excellent form of exercise. It gives the heart, lungs and muscles a good workout, increasing fitness and promoting good health.

Pick Up a Pair

Hello there! You can swap 500 grams of magazines for a pair of eco-friendly chopsticks.

Your magazines weighed 2 kilograms! So you can have four pairs of eco-friendly chopsticks.

Young man, these two pairs of eco-friendly chopsticks are yours.

What's so special about these chopsticks?

You can take them with you wherever you go!

Disposable chopsticks are convenient. Why should I bring my own?

We should use fewer disposable chopsticks, because many trees are cut down in order to make them.

Wash and Reuse

Any regular pair of chopsticks that can be washed and reused can be considered eco-friendly. Make it a habit to say "no" to disposable chopsticks, and carry around your own eco-friendly ones instead.

Pick Up a Pair

Durable and Safe

Most eco-friendly chopsticks are designed to withstand repeated usage. They are made of long-lasting materials such as titanium, stainless steel, alluminium alloys or food-grade plastics.

Benefits of Using
Eco-friendly Chopsticks

Switching to eco-friendly cutlery could help save the environment. Millions of trees and bamboo plants are cut down to make disposable chopsticks. This contributes to deforestation in Asian countries, including China, Vietnam and Indonesia.

Because they are difficult to recycle, disposable chopsticks are single-use and discarded as rubbish. This contributes to problems of waste disposal.

Disposable chopsticks are treated with chemicals that may be harmful to human health. Mould (below) could also grow on disposable chopsticks that remain in storage for long periods of time.

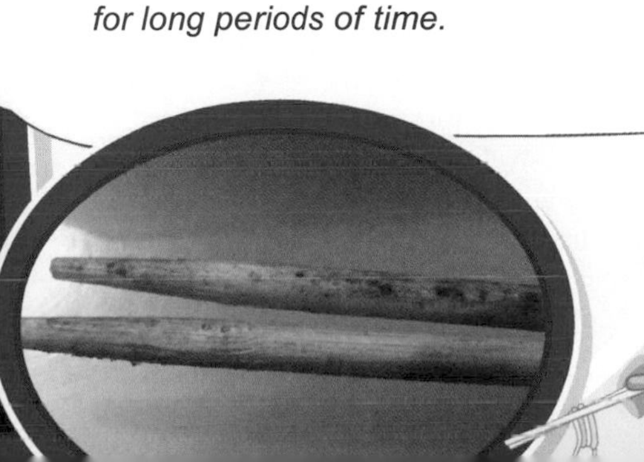

45

Pick Up a Pair

Back to Square Ones

Beep!

Listen up, please!

Our school will be holding a dance contest promoting environmental protection. Our class will use "Less Tissue Paper, More Handkerchiefs" as our theme for the contest.

Why should we use less tissue paper?

Who uses handkerchiefs nowadays?

Using tissues may be convenient and cheap, but they add to the growing problem of rubbish disposal and environmental pollution.

Some types of tissue paper contain fluorescent whitening agents that may be harmful to your body.

Has anyone here ever used scented tissues?

I have. I've used tissue paper with a lavender scent.

Some of the chemical agents added to create scents may cause cancer.

I didn't realise tissue paper had so many hidden dangers.

What are the benefits of replacing tissues with handkerchiefs?

Handkerchiefs can be washed and reused, cutting down on the amount of rubbish we produce.

I'll replace tissues with handkerchiefs from now on!

So will I!

Alright, let's start to learn the dance.

When You're Crying...

A tissue is a thin piece of soft absorbent paper, usually consisting of two or more layers, used for blowing noses, wiping tears, absorbing small spills, and so on. Tissue paper, also known as facial tissue, was invented by the Kleenex company in the 1920s.

Handy Handkerchiefs

It is believed that people began using squares of linen or other cloths to wipe their faces and noses more than 2,000 years ago. Modern handkerchiefs are made of linen, silk or other soft absorbent fabrics, and come in many attractive designs and colours.

Why Should We Use Less Tissue Paper?

Regardless of whether the facial tissue you buy is made from virgin (fresh) or recycled paper pulp, it is still made from the wood of trees. Logging practices contribute to deforestation, and trees take decades to grow back.

Plant pulp is naturally light brown in colour. Most types of tissue paper are whitened with the help of chemical agents such as bleach. This is done to improve their appearance and prolong shelf life. The chemicals, however, can release cancer-causing pollutants, which is bad for the environment as well as our health in the long term.

Paper napkins are usually single-use. Cloth napkins can be used when setting the table, to soak up spills or to cover food. When stained or worn, they can be used as cleaning rags. Natural fibres such as linen can also be decomposed with other organic matter, to make compost.

Bagging It

Not all plastic bags are food safe. Some shouldn't come into contact with hot food.

What? Why not?

High temperatures can soften some plastics. If harmful substances seep from the plastic into the food, it may no longer be safe to eat.

Food bags are made of TPU (thermoplastic polyurethane) or food-grade silicone (a rubberlike material). They are resistant to high temperatures and can hold hot food.

The materials used to make food bags meet the standards of food container testing. It's safe to use these bags.

Cool!

And, unlike plastic bags, food bags are reusable!

51

Bagging It

Portable and Convenient

Food bags are lighter than most food containers. They are easy to carry around because they do not take up much space when empty.

Bagging It

Zack takes out another food bag.

In case we're still hungry…

What do you have there, Zack?

I once went diving and saw many plastic bags floating in the ocean. People are careless about throwing them away!

Hey, Ron, no snatching!

Be careful!

I bet your mum packed us some…

Let's go home and apply some ointment to your scalded finger.

From now on, don't be so greedy.

Oww!! It's hot!

Mum packed hot noodle soup in that food bag.

Roll or Press and Seal

Many food bags are designed to stand upright on their own bases, so that food can be transferred into them easily. Some designs feature a rolled, sealable top that doubles as a handle. Others have ziplock seals.

Benefits of Replacing Plastic Bags with Food Bags

After use, plastic bags are thrown away; they cannot be reused. Food bags, however, can be washed by hand or in a dishwasher. After drying, they are ready to be reused.

A disposable plastic item takes up to hundreds of years to decompose into tiny plastic particles. Replacing single-use plastic bags with reusable food bags helps reduce pollution from plastic waste.

Food bags can help us avoid some of the harmful chemicals in many plastics. For example, phthalates, which are used to make plastic more flexible and are found in food packaging and plastic wrap, have been linked to fertility problems in animal studies. Bisphenol A (BPA), another chemical widely added to food plastics, has been linked to problems with infant development.

New from Old

Berd! Why did you hit me?

I caught you red-handed!

What's wrong with putting recyclables into a regular rubbish bin?

What's wrong with those methods of disposal?

Recycling cuts the size of our landfills in half. Otherwise they would grow closer and closer to where you live.

Unsorted rubbish is either taken to an incinerator for burning or ends up in a landfill, a deep hole where rubbish is buried.

Besides, when we don't recycle, Earth's limited resources disappear faster. Materials such as cardboard, scrap metal, paper and plastic can all be turned into new objects.

Recycling existing products also protects our natural resources and reduces pollution.

Decoding Plastic Symbols

These symbols (right) are commonly found on plastic items. Each number represents a type of plastic, and how it can be recycled. Scan this page and watch the accompanying video to learn more!

1 PETE 2 HDPE 3 V 4 LDPE
5 PP 6 PS 7 OTHER

I'm sorry, Berd. I didn't realise recycling was so beneficial to the environment.

Now you know!

Let's go and put these recyclables in the recycling bins.

Alright! Mum's given me lots of stuff to recycle!

At the recycling station...

Sort the items before you put them in the recycling bins.

Paper has to be put in the blue recycling bin...

The yellow recycling bin is for aluminium cans; the red one is for plastic bottles.

New from Old

What Is Composting?

Composting is a way of helping to break down some kinds of waste. Fruit and vegetable matter and cooked food can all be turned into compost to fertilise gardens.

Berd, what can these recyclables be made into?

Lots of things. For example, recycled paper can be made into pulp to produce paper, tissue, newspapers and other paper products.

Can we tell that a product has been made from recyclables?

Well, products bearing the FSC symbol are certified to have met the sustainable forestry and manufacturing standards of the Forest Stewardship Council.

Aha... I'll keep that in mind.

57

New from Old

The next day...

Mum, is there anything that I can recycle today?

No...

And the next...

Mum, I'm going to recycle this newspaper!

Ryan, come back. That is today's newspaper!

Highest Standards

The Forest Stewardship Council is a non-profit organisation that sets high standards for responsible forestry practices. Products bearing FSC certification, like the playground equipment pictured here, meet the standards of the Forest Stewardship Council in sustainable forest management and environmentally friendly manufacturing practices.

Which Products Are Not Recyclable?

Takeaway Food Containers

Some takeaway foods come in paper or cardboard containers. These containers are not recyclable if they are soiled by grease or food particles. Only clean paper items can be recycled into new products.

Coffee and Bubble Tea Cups

Disposable coffee cups are not recyclable because they are made up of different materials. It is difficult to separate the paper cup from the thin plastic coating on the inside. Also, the plastic used to make coffee cup lids and most bubble tea plastic cups is too low in quality to recycle. If you drink these beverages frequently, invest in your own reusable cup.

Styrofoam

Plastic number 6 is polystyrene, more commonly known by its brand name, Styrofoam. Styrofoam is used to make hot beverage cups and packaging materials. However, it is not recycled locally because the process requires a specialised centre. We should reduce our use of Styrofoam products, and reuse them wherever possible.

Blended to a Pulp

At Uncle Mike's house…

There's no need to throw paper away, even after using both sides.

We can put it in the recycling bins outside, but I've found a way to do my own part for the environment!

What happens after you tear up the paper into little pieces and soak them in water?

Put the soggy pieces into a blender and pulse the blender for about 30 seconds, until the paper becomes a thick paste called pulp.

Pour the pulp into a tub. Add more water and stir the mixture.

Next, put a mould and deckle into the pulp. Gently shake the frame to lay the pulp flat across the mould.

Mould and Deckle

The only special pieces of equipment needed to make recycled paper by hand are a mould and deckle. These are two separate frames of the same size. The mould has a screen attached, to hold the pulp as it drains and dries. The deckle is laid on top of the mould to form the edges of a piece of paper.

Blended to a Pulp

Blended to a Pulp

Colours and Textures

Recycled paper has a distinct appearance. It is usually darker than regular paper because no chemical agents are used to whiten it. It is also coarser in texture. Flecks of colour add interest, making it a popular craft material.

Recycled Paper

Most of the raw materials for recycled paper come from recycled wastepaper, such as newspapers and photocopier paper, which are eco-friendly to produce.

Blended to a Pulp

Commercial papermaking can produce a lot of waste water that pollutes the environment. However, makers of handmade recycled paper can choose processes that are friendlier to the environment.

Many types of packaging paper, notebooks and business cards are made of recycled paper. In the process of making recycled paper, petals, grass and leaves can be added to increase the beauty of the recycled paper.

Plant a Tree

This is your sapling.

Thanks!

Let's plant our sapling here.

Dad, how do trees help improve the environment?

When trees make food in sunlight, they absorb carbon dioxide and release oxygen, purifying the air. This reduces global warming, the rise in Earth's temperature caused by gases that trap heat in the atmosphere.

Trees also give us wood, fruit, shade and shelter. They make the landscape look beautiful too.

Trees are so important!

Plant a Tree

Dedicated to Tree Planting

Many countries all over the world observe a day or more dedicated to planting and celebrating trees. In the Netherlands, the National Tree Festival falls on 22 March. The United Kingdom celebrates National Tree Week at the start of tree-planting season in November.

I hope the saplings grow fast and turn this empty space into a forest.

As more people become aware of environmental protection and take part in tree-planting activities, our living environment will be greatly improved.

Hey, there's Eric!

Eric!

Kade! You're planting a tree too!

Let me see what wish you've made...

No!

Ha ha! Eric's wish is to be able to eat chicken drumsticks every day.

Hey, that wish was private and confidential!

Important Ecosystems

Forests are home to many plants and animals that would not survive in any other habitat. Afforestation (the practice of planting a large number of trees on empty land) helps prevent soil erosion and create new ecosystems.

Benefits of Afforestation

Afforestation prevents soil and its nutrients from being washed away by the rain. Trees also reduce the speed and force of the wind across empty land and sand dunes, helping to stabilise sand dunes and slow down wind erosion of the coast.

In sunlight, trees make food by absorbing carbon dioxide from the air and releasing oxygen. As a result, afforestation can purify the air we breathe.

Planting trees in areas that were previously not productive provides people with a source of tree products and a peaceful, pleasant environment to enjoy.

Plant a Tree

From Food Scraps to Fertiliser

Food waste and certain fabrics made from plant fibre can be made into organic fertiliser. Then we don't have to buy it.

Banana peel is a common organic fertiliser that I use.

What advantages does it have?

Banana peel is rich in phosphorus and potassium. This promotes plant growth and the blooming of flowers.

Besides, it's odourless.

What other materials can be used to make organic fertilisers?

Livestock and poultry manures, such as cow and chicken droppings, can also be made into organic fertilisers.

Fresh droppings do stink, and there is a risk that any parasites in the droppings could infest the compost pile. So I prefer not to compost droppings.

I see.

Phew!

Don't the droppings smell terrible and spread disease?

Organic Fertiliser

An organic fertiliser is made by decomposing natural plant or animal matter, usually with the help of microorganisms such as bacteria. Most kitchen waste can be processed into organic fertiliser.

From Food Scraps to Fertiliser

68

I've baked the banana peels on low heat until they are dried and blackened. Now you can crumble them and apply the fertiliser to the soil outside!

The use of organic fertilisers can reduce the pollution caused by chemical fertilisers.

And waste is reused, reducing the amount of rubbish piling up in the landfills.

Aunty Rachel, teach us a few more methods of making organic fertiliser.

We will want to try doing that when we get home.

No problem. You just have to help me pluck out all the weeds first.

Growing Better Gardens

The application of organic fertilisers can effectively improve soil structure, helping the soil retain water and nutrients longer. Organic fertilisers also feed the microorganisms in soil, helping them make even more nutrients for plants.

Compost and Other Organic Fertilisers

Composting is the process of recycling organic material, such as leaves, vegetable scraps and food waste, into fertilisers. It is a great way to reduce waste and contributions to greenhouse gas emissions from the burning of rubbish.

From Food Scraps to Fertiliser

What items can be turned into compost? Almost anything plant-based: tea leaves; herbs or spices; fruit seeds, rinds, skins, husks or cores; vegetable peels; stale bread; expired cereal or pasta; coffee grounds and filters are all acceptable. But avoid putting meat or dairy products into a home compost, because they attract pests. Also avoid oil and grease, which slow down the decomposition process.

A green manure is an organic fertiliser that is made from cultivated or wild green plants. Green manures are rich in nutrients. After decomposition, they can increase organic matter and trace elements, such as phosphorus, potassium and calcium, in soil.

Here Comes the Sun

Star Power

The sun is a star whose energy radiates across space to our planet, reaching Earth in the form of light and heat. Solar energy can also be converted into electricity.

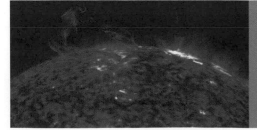

All we have to do is convert sunlight into electricity.

How does the conversion process work?

The solar power bank contains a solar cell (or photovoltaic cell) consisting of two different materials. When sunlight falls on the cell, it delivers energy to tiny negatively charged particles called electrons. The electrons move, creating a negative voltage on the surface facing the sun, and a positive voltage on the rear surface. The front and rear surfaces can be connected to extract an electric current from the solar cell.

Sunlight

Light bulb lights up

Negative electrode

Positive electrode

Electric current

73

Here Comes the Sun

If there are more solar cells, will more energy be generated?

Yes.

Solar chargers with one panel, like this one, are more compact, but they also convert the sun's energy more slowly.

Power banks with multiple panels can speed things up a bit but are often bulkier and heavier.

Calculate This!
Photovoltaic cells work with artificial light sources as well as sunlight. However, their energy output is higher with sunlight than artificial light. A solar-powered calculator can work without batteries, because it generates electricity with the help of solar panels.

Here Comes the Sun

Switching to Solar Energy

The cost of manufacturing solar panels has fallen dramatically in the last decade, making them more affordable. At the same time, technological advances have improved their efficiency. In countries like Australia and Germany, they are growing in popularity among homeowners.

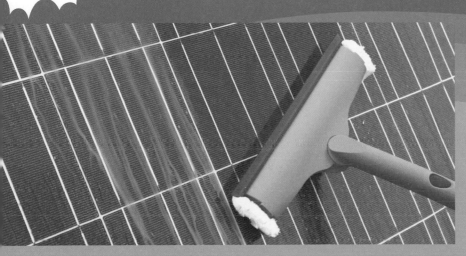

Gas and oil are nonrenewable natural resources. Once they are used up, we will have to find alternative ways of generating electricity.

Solar energy is a renewable resource – sunlight is constantly replenished and doesn't run out. Solar energy has many eco-friendly benefits. It is plentiful and does not generate noise or produce chemicals that harm the environment.

Here Comes the Sun

Solar products do not need much maintenance. Once installed, a solar panel is expected to last about 30 years. All it requires is light cleaning to make sure dirt, leaves and other objects are not obstructing the panel.

Poo-wer Generator

Electricity is indispensable in our daily lives. We generate electricity by using fossil fuels (coal, oil and natural gas), hydro-energy, solar power and wind power. But did you ever think that faeces could be used to generate electricity? Let's find out more!

Faeces is the solid waste passed out by humans or animals. Since it contains organic matter, including microorganisms, minerals and other nutrients that plants need, it is often used as fertiliser in agriculture.

However, with the rapid development of better-smelling, more hygienic fertilisers, faeces has declined in popularity as an agricultural fertiliser. Faeces has now become a waste problem that needs to be dealt with.

Human waste is processed and cleansed at wastewater treatment plants, but animal waste from farms has turned into a huge problem.

Large amounts of animal waste represent a pollution hazard. The smell is foul, and methane, a greenhouse gas, is produced in large quantities when animal waste decomposes.

Unprocessed faeces flows into and pollutes rivers, lakes and other waterways. The nutrients in faeces can fuel uncontrolled algae growth. At night, the algae absorbs oxygen from the water, and can cause fish and other aquatic creatures to die off in large numbers.

77

Poo-wer Generator

Consuming water that is contaminated with faecal matter can spread diseases such as cholera and typhoid.

In recent years, scientists have discovered one solution to the problem of poo – human and animal faeces can be used to generate electricity!

BIOWASTE AND
ORGANIC WASTE

BIOGAS
Output

Inlet

Outlet

BIODIGESTER

BIOFERTILIZER
AND SLUDGE

78

Poo-wer Generator

To produce electricity from waste matter, organic material (human excrement, animal droppings and food waste) is collected and fed into a container known as a biodigester.

In the biodigester, special bacteria decomposes the organic waste in an oxygen-free (anaerobic) environment to produce a renewable energy called biogas (methane and carbon dioxide). Biogas is used to fuel generators to produce electricity.

After the biogas is removed, faecal residue from the biodigestion process can be turned into a variety of useful products, including organic fertiliser, livestock bedding, compost, fuel pellets and construction materials.

SHRI (Sanitation and Health Rights in India) is an organisation that aims to end the practice of defecating in the open, by building public toilets for people in India. Methane gas produced from the waste collected in the toilets is used to power a water filtration system that provides clean water to villages.

The Blue Spruce Farm in Vermont, United States, is one of the first farms in the world to harness the renewable energy potential of cow manure. On the farm, biogas produced by animal waste is converted into enough electricity for more than 300 homes in the community.

79

Poo-wer Generator

Britain's first street lamp powered by dog poo is located in the Malvern Hills, England. When dog poo is collected and placed inside the device and the handle rotated, the device heats up and stirs the poo with microorganisms in an oxygen-free chamber, so that methane gas is released and used to light up the lamp. About 10 bags of poo are sufficient to keep the lamp lit for 2 hours.

Organic waste is a practical source of renewable energy. Using organic waste to generate electricity can reduce our consumption of nonrenewable forms of energy. It can also hygienically dispose of this waste and prevent problems such as water pollution.

So, How Much Do You Really Know About the Green Movement?

Challenge yourself to recall key moments of your Adventures in the Green Movement, and find out where you rank on the Environ-meter!

Get ready, get set, scan!

ENVIRON-METER

10	Certified Conservationist! Congratulations, we're impressed!
9–8	Enthusiastic Ecologist! Great job!
7–6	Go Greener! Try again!
5–4	Friend of the Environment? You can do better!
3–0	What Planet Are You On? Help save this one!

80

Where do germs live?
Why is plastic waste harmful?
Which animals have winter coats?
What is the darkest known material?
How do barcodes work?

Introducing the sensational new *World of Science* comics series designed specially for inquiring young minds! Experience Science come alive through dynamic, full-colour comics enriched by Augmented Reality.

Books in this series so far:
- *Birds*
- *Plants and Fungi*
- *Insects*
- *Aquatic Creatures*
- *Human Body*
- *Land Animals*
- *Reptiles and Amphibians*
- *Natural Wonders*
- *How Things Work*
- *Great Minds*
- *Germs and Your Health*
- *Green Movement*
- *More Land Animals*
- *Materials*
- *Technology and Gadgets*

Look out for *Endangered Animals, Useful Plants and Fungi, More Materials, More Natural Wonders, Discoveries and Inventions,* and many more!

To receive updates about children's titles from WS Education, go to https://www.worldscientific.com/page/newsletter/subscribe, choose "Education", click on "Children's Books" and key in your email address. Follow us @worldscientificedu on Instagram and @World Scientific Education on YouTube for our